DATE DUE

DEMCO 38-297

GYPSIES

ELIZABETH SIRIMARCO

SMART APPLE MEDIA MANKATO MINNESOTA

Published by Smart Apple Media
123 South Broad Street, Mankato, Minnesota 56001

Copyright © 2000 Smart Apple Media.
International copyrights reserved in all countries.
No part of this book may be reproduced in any form without written
permission from the publisher.

Produced by The Creative Spark, San Juan Capistrano, CA
    Editor: Elizabeth Sirimarco
    Designer: Mary Francis-DeMarois
    Art Direction: Robert Court
    Page Layout: Janine Graham

Photos/Illustrations: Carlos Humberto T.D.C/Contact Press Images/PNI 4;
Chris Hellier/ Corbis 6; B. Gy. Medgyasszay/Sovfoto/Eastfoto/PNI 7;
Dorothy Littell/Stock, Boston/PNI 8-9; G. Udovichenko/Sovfoto/Eastfoto/
PNI 10; Kevin Davidson 12; Nick Wheeler/Corbis 14; Barry Lewis ©
Corbis 16; Ann Purcell 18; Carl Purcell/Words & Pictures/PNI; Library of
Congress/Corbis 20; V. Khristoforov/Sovfoto/Eastfoto/PNI 21; Courtesy of
the United States Holocaust Memorial Museum 22; Rick Gerharter/Impact
Visuals/PNI 25; Martin Gust/Sovfoto/Eastfoto/PNI 26; Reuters/ Liukas
Unseld/Archive Photos 29

Library of Congress Cataloging-in-Publication Data
Sirimarco, Elizabeth, 1966–
    Gypsies / by Elizabeth Sirimarco.
        p. cm. — (Endangered cultures)
    Includes bibliographical references and index.
    Summary: Details the origin, history, occupations, language,
special names, clothing and other customs of gypsies, as well as
their persecution, current status, and struggle to preserve their
culture and identity.
    ISBN 1-887068-91-0
    1. Gypsies—Juvenile literature. [1. Gypsies.] I. Title. II. Series.
DX118.S585 1999
305.891'497—dc21   98-36422

First edition

9   8   7   6   5   4   3   2   1

Table of Contents

A Gypsy family in South America sits together in a makeshift tent. In recent years, the majority of Gypsies around the world have settled into homes in big cities, but a small portion are still nomadic for all or part of the year. Others are simply too poor to afford proper housing.

Gypsies Today

The word gypsy is often used to mean a **nomad,** or any person who travels from place to place and does not have a fixed home. Gypsies, however, are a true ethnic group. They have their own language and their own history. There are at least 12 million Gypsies, also known as **Roma,** living all around the world, but some estimates suggest that as of 1998, there were 15 million Gypsies in Europe alone. Obtaining accurate information about the Roma can be difficult because they are a secretive and isolated group.

Folk tales depict Gypsies as exotic, dark-skinned people who wear colorful clothing and weave golden coins in their hair. Non-Gypsies often imagine that the Roma travel in brightly decorated wooden carts. Gypsies may perform lively music or circus stunts. Sometimes they might train animals, such as bears or monkeys, to dance for money. Perhaps they tell fortunes.

Not all of these typical images of Gypsies are untrue. Some Gypsies are nomads, but today most spend their lives in settlements with their extended families. Some Gypsies do wear the full, colorful skirts, the head scarves, and the golden earrings depicted in books and movies. More often, Gypsies wear modern clothing, perhaps the hand-me-downs of non-Gypsies.

The Roma migrate from northwest India to Persia.

The Ursari, which means "bear leaders," are a tribe of Gypsies primarily found in Eastern Europe. They are well known for training bears to do tricks and perform for crowds. Records indicate they have worked with these animals since at least the seventh century, but now only a small number of Ursari actually train bears.

Some Gypsies make their living performing traditional folk music. Others read the palms of the *gadje,* their word for anyone who is not a Gypsy. More often, Gypsies are traders, metal workers, or craftsmen. Unfortunately, many are not employed at all, and many live in poverty.

Gypsies have traveled through many lands with very different cultures, picking up pieces of language and tradition as they moved on. They have few customs or beliefs that are common to all groups or tribes. They have no religion that is typical of their people, although they may adopt the religion of a place where they settle.

Gypsies also have no instrument or sound that is identical in all tribes, even though they have long been known for their musical talents. The music they play is often influenced by their environment. If they support themselves and their families with song, they play what

C. 1300

The Roma arrive in Europe. They are considered outsiders because they are a non-Christian, non-white people who have no territory of their own on the continent.

Song and dance have long been important to Gypsy culture, although their music is frequently influenced by the countries in which they settle.

Some Gypsy women still dress according to tradition. For example, they wear long, colorful skirts because it is considered improper for a woman to show her legs. Head scarves are called *dikló* and are worn by married women.

1510

France begins to enact laws to keep the Roma from entering the country. Roma who do so are whipped or beaten.

In the past, many Gypsies could not read or write, so they relied on verbal histories told by elders to pass on their history. Even today, many Roma are illiterate, in part because of the belief that it prevents the ideas and values of the gadje *from influencing Gypsy life.*

the audience finds most pleasing. Gypsies in Hungary may play that country's folk music on violins or small accordions called concertinas. Gypsies in Spain perform a traditional dance known as flamenco, accompanied by fast, rhythmic music played on the guitar.

There are some common traits among Gypsies, however. They are expected to have very limited contact with *gadje*, avoiding them except in business dealings. They consider non-Gypsies dangerous and *marimé*, or unclean.

Gypsies have many other rules about what is clean and what is unclean and are very much afraid of **contamination**. Around the world, they share beliefs about such things as what may be eaten and how to wash oneself. These codes of behavior strictly define interaction between male and female, Gypsy and *gadje*. The clothing of men and women must be washed separately. Food prepared by *gadje* is *marimé* and can contaminate a Gypsy who eats it.

Another common custom is the burning of the home and belongings of a dead family member. Gypsies fear that the spirit of the dead may linger to haunt the living. Destroying his or her belongings will safeguard those who live on after the dead.

1589

Denmark decrees that any Gypsy leader found in that country would be sentenced to death.

Secret Signs

The word *patrin* means "leaf" or "page" in the Romani language. It also refers to markers that traveling Roma would leave behind so other Gypsies could find them. Sometimes *patrin* were used to pass on news, using signals that only other tribe members could understand. A *patrin* might be some twigs tied together with a red string or perhaps a branch broken in a particular way.

SCOTLAND
1447

ARCTIC OCEAN

ATLANTIC OCEAN

ENGLAND
1430s

SWEDEN
1515

SPAIN
1425

FRANCE
1419

GERMANY
1407

BALTIC SEA

SWITZERLAND
1414

POLAND
1428

RUSSIA
1500

ITALY
1422

SERBIA
1348

M E D I T E R R A N E A N   S E A

BLACK SEA

CASPIAN
SEA

CRETE
1322

TURKEY
1050

IRAN (PERSIA)
Pre-1000

INDIA

BALKAN PENINSULA
1370s

CROATIA

HUNGARY

BOSNIA

SERBIA

ROMANIA

ALBANIA

MACEDONIA

GREECE

BULGARIA

AEGEAN
SEA

BLACK
SEA

Mysterious Past, Silent History

The Gypsies have lived in Europe for many hundreds of years—so long that until recently, no one was sure where they came from. Gypsies themselves did not keep any records, nor did they think of themselves as a special group or race. Many are still unaware that people who look like them—who even speak the same language—live in countries all around the world.

From approximately the 15th century until well into the 19th century, it was believed that Gypsies came from Egypt. Europeans called them "Little Egyptians," from which came the English word Gypsy. Gypsies call themselves Roma. Most Roma speak a language known as **Romani.** (Romani is also an adjective that means of or relating to the Roma.) Because Gypsies live in so many different countries, there are regional variations in pronunciation, vocabulary, and sentence structure, called **dialects.**

It wasn't until the 18th century that European anthropologists, scientists who study human beings and their

The map at left shows a possible migratory route of the Roma from Northwest India to Persia, and finally into Europe. The dates show the first recorded presence of the Gypsies in a country, but the Roma may have been present earlier.

1721

German ruler Karl VI orders the murder of all Roma. "Gypsy Hunts" are held.

origins, studied the Roma. It seemed that perhaps these people, who looked so different from other Europeans, might be from India. The unfamiliar language they spoke was what helped solve the mystery.

Anthropologists first made a list of Romani words. Then it was compared to two Indian languages, Hindi and Sanskrit. The connection between the languages was clear. In fact, the comparison showed that one in three words were similar. Scientists began to realize that Gypsies must have migrated to Europe from India.

Gypsies have no myths about the beginning of the world. They do not tell stories about their homeland and often know little about the origin of their people. Throughout their history, most Gypsies were **illiterate** and couldn't record the tales of their elders. In addition, Roma have chosen to remain isolated from the *gadje* and do not offer freely whatever they may know about their past. Anthropologists used the histories of other peoples to piece together the puzzle of the Romani past. Unfortunately, this has meant that the information available is not always accurate.

It is believed that from India, the Gypsies first arrived in Persia, which is now called Iran. Persian legend says that in the fifth century, a king named Bahram Gur decided his subjects should have music to entertain them. He asked the king of India

Gypsies have lived in many lands over the centuries. Anthropologists have learned that they originally came from India.

A Common Origin

Following are a few words in English, Sanskrit, Hindi, and Romani. Notice the similarity between the two Indian languages and Romani.

ENGLISH	SANSKRIT	HINDI	ROMANI
man	manusa	manusya	manus
sun	gharma	gham	kham
nose	nakka	nak	nakh
water	paniya	pani	pai
you	tuvam	tu	tu

1761

The Queen of Hungary tries to turn the Roma into what she calls "New Hungarians." They are given tools, seeds, and animals to set up farms. The Romani language is outlawed, and nomadic communities are forced to settle.

to send him musicians. The Indian ruler responded by sending 12,000 men, women, and children.

Bahram Gur sent the musicians to live throughout his kingdom. He gave them grain and cattle so they would be able to support themselves. A year later, he learned that the musicians had eaten all the grain, as well as the cattle. He became very angry and said they must now travel the land, finding whatever work they could. From then on, legend says, the Indian musicians roamed the countryside playing music and trading horses, stealing coins and telling fortunes.

No one knows exactly when the Gypsies arrived in Persia, or how long it took them to move through the Middle East into Europe. By the 15th century, they had traveled as far west as England. By the 19th century, Gypsies, like others from Europe, were migrating to North and South America.

Roma often make their homes in settlements away from other residents of the cities and towns where they live. One reason Gypsies live apart is the belief that it keeps their special customs alive, but they are frequently unwelcome in the communities of non-Gypsies.

An Unwelcome People

Gypsies are often victims of **prejudice,** and many people fear them simply because they are different. Non-gypsies accuse the Roma of being thieves and beggars, even though only a small number actually participate in such activities. Gypsies sometimes live in poor conditions, so it is believed that they are dirty or spread disease. These **stereotypes** are not new. Gypsies have lived as outsiders for hundreds of years.

Over the years, Gypsies were occasionally welcomed to European towns and villages. In the 15th century, Eastern Europeans appreciated the Gypsies for their skills as craftsmen and metal workers. Into the 19th century, the most talented Gypsy musicians were fought over in much of Europe because their music was a favorite of kings and noblemen. Gypsy dancers and acrobats frequently performed for large, happy crowds.

A more common theme in the history of the Gypsies is **persecution.** Europeans usually lived in the same place for their whole lives. Gypsies seemed dangerous because they were always on the move. Villagers believed that they roamed the countryside in search of new places to beg for food, clothing, and money so they would not have to work. Others claimed that Gypsies traveled about

Roma have practiced fortune telling for many centuries as a means to make money from the gadje, *although they do not believe in such powers themselves. Gypsy fortune tellers, called* drabardi *in Romani, are always women.*

because they were thieves—staying in one place for too long would increase the risk of being caught.

Many Christians believed the Gypsies' well-known talent for fortune telling and palm reading was the work of the devil. In places where the Roma were known as horse traders, natives claimed they were experts at cheating people by making a sick or lame animal appear to be in good condition. They often were falsely suspected of being spies. Some people claimed Gypsies spread the bubonic plague, a disease that killed at least one-fourth of the European population during the 14th century. The plague was actually spread by rodents and insects.

Very soon after the Gypsies arrived in a country, villagers and townspeople began to complain about them. Their dark skin and unusual clothing seemed strange. They spoke a language no one else could understand. Sometimes Gypsies took money and food from people who did not have very much themselves.

Wherever the Gypsies were unwelcome, people created laws forcing them to leave, although they had no homeland to which they could return. Some Gypsies were nomads not by choice, but because they were unable to find a place where natives would allow them to settle.

Laws were enacted all across Europe that allowed Roma children to be taken from their parents and raised by Christians. Gypsies in France were branded, and their heads were shaved so that they would be easy to recognize. Because it was the Gypsy women who were most frequently accused of theft, their ears were cut off in parts of Eastern Europe so people would know to be wary of them.

1864

The enslavement of Gypsies is made illegal in Romania.

CURSED BY GOD?

Some people say the Roma have been persecuted throughout history because they are cursed by God. One story says that a Gypsy metal worker forged the nails that were used to crucify Jesus Christ. Another legend claims that they are the descendants of Cain, the son of Adam and Eve who killed his brother.

1888

The Gypsy Lore Society is founded by non-Gypsies to gather scholarly information.

The habits and appearance of the Gypsies have always been different. This often has made them the victims of prejudice and persecution.

In Germany, Gypsies were beaten and branded. They could also be forced out of the country—even if they had committed no crime. If they returned, it was legal to kill them.

In the former kingdom of Prussia, all Gypsies over the age of 18 were hung, and sometimes a reward was offered to those who captured them. Sweden decreed

20

that all Gypsy males were to be hanged. In Holland, Gypsies were hunted like animals, and hunters were often rewarded for killing them.

Until the 19th century, Gypsies were kept as slaves in what is now Romania. They were considered to be the property of their owners. When young women were married, Gypsy slaves were often part of their **dowry,** and sons would inherit whole families of slaves from their fathers. Gypsy families were often separated from one another when they were sold or given away to other owners.

The enslavement of Gypsies was made illegal in 1864, but anti-Gypsy laws would never completely disappear.

1933 – 1945

Between 500,000 and one million Roma are killed by the Nazis during the Holocaust.

Throughout history, Gypsy women and children have begged for money to supplement income the men earned by metal working or other crafts. The practice of begging may have started when Romani women were sent out to collect payment for the work of their husbands.

21

A group of Romani prisoners sits in an open area of the Belzec concentration camp in Poland, awaiting instructions from their Nazi captors.

Troubled Century

Well into the 20th century, European countries were still trying to figure out how to solve "the Gypsy problem." While laws were less severe than they had been in the past, some countries made it illegal to live as a nomad. Sometimes Gypsies were forced to register with authorities when they arrived in a city and then carry special documents with them at all times. Much worse treatment was on the way.

In 1933, the Nazi party, led by Adolf Hitler, came to power in Germany. The Nazis did not believe that all human beings had the same rights. They wanted to preserve what they considered a perfect German race and remove all non-Germans from their country. They also wanted to gain control of the rest of Europe so that their beliefs would be recognized elsewhere. Other countries did not want Germany to have such great power, and World War II broke out.

The Nazis aimed to rid their country of certain types of people. They decided the only way to accomplish this was to put them in **concentration camps**. Only two groups of people were captured solely because of their race: the Jews and the Gypsies.

1971

The first World Romani Congress is held in London.

Like the Jews, Gypsies were brought to cramped, dirty concentration camps. Once there, they were starved, forced to do hard labor, used for medical experiments, or murdered. The slaughter of millions of people by the Nazis during World War II is known as the **Holocaust.**

The Romani word for the Gypsy Holocaust is *Porraimos* (pronounced paw-Rye-mos), which means "The Devouring." Not many Roma know this word, in part because they know very little of what happened to their people during World War II. Romani survivors seldom spoke of their terrible experiences. History books written by non-Gypsies virtually ignore the fact that the Roma were victims of the Holocaust.

The latest estimate is that between 500,000 and one million Gypsies were killed during the Holocaust, yet few people are aware of it. Germany paid **reparation** money—funds given as an apology for wrongdoing—to Jewish survivors of the Holocaust. No money was ever given to Romani survivors. Hundreds of millions of dollars were made available to victims of the Nazis by the United Nations. Only 10 percent of this money went to non-Jews, and none of it went to the Roma. The *Porraimos* is a forgotten holocaust.

World War II ended in 1945, and the Nazis were removed from power. Eastern Europe then came under communist rule. Communist policy states that all people should be equal. No one should have more money than someone else, and there should be no differences in religion or traditions. The government imposed strict guidelines on most aspects of people's lives.

More than ever, Gypsies were discouraged from their nomadic lifestyle. Communist governments forced the

Roma to settle in European neighborhoods. They were told to take non-Gypsy names and work in the community. The governments believed "the Gypsy problem" could be solved simply by taking away the things that made them different.

Unfortunately, no one was happy with the arrangement. The local people wanted their cities and towns to be the same as they always had been. The Gypsies wanted little to do with the *gadje*. Nonetheless, they managed to live in relative peace during the communist years. Both the Roma and the *gadje* were afraid of being punished if they did not live as the government told them to. Then, in 1989, communist rule of Eastern Europe ended, creating different problems for Europeans to solve and renewing persecution of the Roma.

1979

The Romani people are recognized as a distinct race by the United Nations.

At least 21,000 Gypsies were killed at the Auschwitz concentration camp between February 1943 and August 1944.

In the Czech Republic, more than 300 demonstrators gathered on January 30, 1994—the 60th anniversary of Hitler's rise to power. Some carried signs that read, "Gypsies belong in the gas chamber," referring to the way that many victims were killed during the Holocaust.

Opré Roma!

As Eastern Europe enters the new millennium, jobs are difficult to find. There is a lot of competition for work, and citizens often resent those who seem to be doing well. Many Europeans believe that Gypsies are taking away their jobs. They also believe that anyone who does not work must be stealing and swindling.

Since 1989, there has been a sharp increase in violence directed toward Gypsies. Gypsy settlements have been burned to the ground, leaving hundreds of families without roofs over their heads. In Romania alone, there were 35 serious attacks on Gypsy settlements between 1989 and 1995. With each attack, people seemed to be less concerned. Romanian newspapers have seldom reported crimes committed against the Gypsies.

Life can be difficult for Gypsies in Western Europe as well. In Austria, four Roma were killed by a pipe bomb in 1995. The bomb was hidden behind a sign that read "Gypsies Go Back to India." The Roma were trying to take the sign down when the bomb exploded.

Germans protest the arrival of Gypsies who come to their country looking for work. More than 200 Roma were killed when a bomb exploded in a German hostel in 1992.

1989

Communist
governments fall
in Eastern Europe.
Attacks on
Roma increase
dramatically.

In that same year, 1,163 racial crimes were reported in a single month in German cities and towns.

Fortunately, there are movements to help the Roma. Organizations have been formed in the hope of uniting Gypsies from around the world and creating a means to protect them.

In 1971, the first World Romani Congress was held in London. Gypsies from 14 countries participated. It was at this meeting that the term Roma was first used, derived from the word *rom*, which means "free person" in Romani. They also designed a flag. *Opré Roma* (Gypsy Arise) became the motto of the Roma people. Small groups were organized to deal with concerns about social affairs, education, war crimes, language, and culture. Roma from 25 different countries attended the next World Romani Congress.

The International Romani Union was established when the United Nations (UN) finally recognized the Roma as a distinct racial group in 1979. In 1993, the Union was granted voting rights within the UN, giving the Roma a voice in the international community for the first time in history. Today the International Romani Union continues to work for the rights of the Roma. Perhaps its most important goal is to provide a unified force to help Roma who have suffered, and continue to suffer, human-rights abuses.

Future goals of the Union are to establish a standard Romani language and to create a Romani encyclopedia written especially for Gypsies, not just about them. The encyclopedia will help Roma reshape what they know of their past. It will also help non-Gypsies better understand Romani culture and history. The Union also hopes to bring to light information about the *Porraimos*.

Another goal is to provide protection to Roma who are still being persecuted now.

Unfortunately, an estimated 50 percent of Gypsies remain illiterate, and the majority are unemployed. Their lives are about one-third shorter than non-Gypsies who live in the same regions. Many live in inadequate housing. The end of the 20th century, however, has brought new hope. In the past, Gypsies were a powerless minority who lived in small groups. There was no one to look out for them, no one to recognize how unjustly they were treated. For the first time in history, the Roma have begun to unite and form a common voice. As Roma leaders struggle to make other Roma recognize the value of their distinct heritage, it may also be recognized by the world.

1994

Delegates from the International Romani Union testify before the United States Congress about the abuses suffered by the Roma.

Ernst Wagner sits solemnly with his wife and two daughters at a 1998 ceremony during which he and two other Gypsies received symbolic reparation payments from the Swiss Holocaust Memorial Fund. Wagner, a Holocaust survivor, is part of the International Romani Union, which is demanding compensation equal to that given other Holocaust victims.

Glossary

concentration camps
Places where prisoners of war are confined. During World War II, victims of the Holocaust were taken to such camps to be killed.

contamination
The act of becoming dirty or impure by contact with something.

dialects
Regional differences in a language, such as variances in pronunciation, vocabulary, and sentence structure.

dowry
Money or goods that a woman's family gives to her new husband when they marry.

gadje
The Romani word for non-Gypsies.

Holocaust
The attempted extermination of different groups of people, including Jews, Gypsies, the handicapped, the mentally ill, and others by the Nazis during World War II.

illiterate
Unable to read or write.

nomad
An individual who travels from place to place and does not have a fixed home.

persecution
The practice of harassing or attacking an individual or group, usually because they are of a different origin, religion, or race.

prejudice	A bad feeling or opinion about something or someone without just reason; a feeling of anger toward a group or its characteristics.
reparation	Funds given as an apology for wrongdoing, such as those offered to certain victims of the Holocaust.
Roma	Another word for Gypsy. The term was coined by attendees of the first World Romani Congress in 1971.
Romani	Of or relating to the Roma. Also, the language spoken by Romani people.
stereotypes	Standard, overly simple ideas of what something, such as a group of people, is like.

Further Reading and Information

BOOKS:
Tong, Diane. *Gypsy Folktales*. New York, NY: Fine Commun., 1997.
Leland, Charles Godfrey. *Gypsy Sorcery and Fortune Telling*.
    Secaucus, NJ: Citadel Press, 1990.

WEB SITES:
http://www.geocities.com/Paris/5121/patrin.htm

VIDEO:
Latcho Drom (New Yorker Video), depicts the traditional music and
    dance of Roma in various countries around the world.

Index

Items in bold print indicate illustration.